HOTCHPOTCH

A little bit of this , A little bit of that

Bhagavath Krishna

/ BookLeaf
Publishing

India | USA | UK

Made with ❤ on the BookLeaf Publishing Platform
www.bookleafpub.in
www.bookleafpub.com

Dedication

To Ammachi and Appa,

With deepest love and gratitude, I dedicate this work to
you both. Holding your hands, I saw the beauty of
nature.
In Appa's arms, I felt on top of the world and in
Ammachi's lap, I found greatest comfort. Your words,
stories, songs, tasty food and unconditional love
nurtured my senses and shaped my soul.
As I step into the world of writing, though inexperienced
and imperfect, I'm humbled by your love and support.
Each letter, each line I wrote , is a reflection of the
memories and values you've instilled in me.
May your blessings guide me as I embark on this
journey. This work, and all that follows, is a token of my
love and appreciation for you both.

Preface

Hotchpotch is like a big box of colorful things! It's a mix of everything I saw, heard, and felt.
A mixture of little observations and experiences, genuine insights, and random topics that stretch across India's culture and diversity. Love, impermanence, wonder, hopes, and ambitions all find a space here. When you read it, I hope you'll smile and feel happy too!

Acknowledgements

To Achan and Amma....

I owe a debt of gratitude for your unwavering support and love. You've been the wind beneath my wings, turning my dreams into reality.Our long drives and chai-fueled conversations, devoid of stills and photography, yet rich in laughter and stories, have been the catalyst for this work. I'll cherish these moments forever. Thank you for being my guiding lights. I hope these poems bring a smile to your faces and warmth to your hearts.

1. A DEMOCRATIC RECIPE

In the bubbling pot of sambhar,
Stories of India gently stir,
Where tamarind sings of tangy South,
And spices dance with fiery mouth.

Drumstick, tall like temple towers,
From southern land it gains its powers;
Brinjal, purple royal shade,
Echoes Deccan's grand parade.

Bhindi from the fields of Bengal,
Slender, green, yet standing tall;
Carrot bright from Punjab plains,
Golden sun in farmer's gains.

Pumpkin sweet from Kerala's shore,
Whispers myths of folklore;
Tomato red, from everywhere,
Like the people's vibrant care.

Onion rings from Gujarat spin,
Circles of trade, spice within;
Lentils steady, pulses strong,
Bind the broth, like bonds lifelong.

Curry leaves, fragrant, free,
Carry South's rich melody;
Mustard seeds, when they explode,
Are fireworks on the festive road.

Together they simmer, none apart,
Each with a role, yet one in heart;
Just as India, vast and wide,
Finds her strength where culture's unite.

So taste the sambhar, rich and deep,
In every spoon, a pledge we keep:
That many voices, hues and lands,
Are one when joined by loving hands.

2. CHECKMATE

In black and white, a zebra's stripe

I ponder, which color will rule.

Is it black over white or white over black?

A Question that echoes, with no clear track.

This Puzzle stretches to 64 squares,

Where Chess, my favorite Sport unfolds.

A real battle rages with PLAN B,

BE ALERT – the motto be.

The knight jumps high like a bunny in space,

The rook's straight drive shakes the race,

The bishop slides with sneaky grin,

Queen, The All Rounder always wins

And Pawn tries its best.

Yet, amidst this thoughtful play

I wonder who designed the majestic sway,

The king who hides when others take the fall.

Its like a traffic Jam, with all the pieces around

Be careful not to get knocked down!

In black and white, the game's a test

Of Wit and Will, the best shines with delight.

3. PAPER BOAT

Oh ! the frog is croaking ....
yeah its time for
rain.......
Suddenly ''Tip Tip Barsa Pani ''.................
hmmm... the smell of the sand , I love it ,
its really enchanting .
I love the smell of sand and old
books.

I thought of that dear "Natural Weaver "SPIDER weaving
his cobweb throughout the day .
The naughty raindrops ...
destroyed his grand marvel.

I sat in the veranda ,
enjoyed rain with a cup of kattan chaya...
I could see the magical moves of Michael Jackson in
Raindrops ,
when they touched
the Earth .

Somewhere doing the Anti GRAVITY lean
and others spinning and back sliding with the
direction of the wind .

I made a paper
boat .. but in the heavy rain , my paper boat met
with a great mishap which No Titanic might have
met.

Thank God no Jack and Jill were on board .
Sometimes I feel like going out in the heavy rain
and dance and jump in the muddy
puddles like Peppa Pig .

But when I see lightning
and thunderstorm, I sit in inside and pat my self..
...Are bhai ALL IS WELL ....
it's a racing held between Light and Sound in
which Sound has not yet defeated Light .
I just can't believe ,
How Benjamin Franklin did the
famous – KITE IN THUNDERSTORM experiment .

How funny is that he found it as the perfect time
to do an experiment .

When I was small kid now not that young ... I

thought that Lightning and Thunder are
PIKACHU'S special moves ...
and I wished to have
to reddish circle on my cheeks to store electricity
and do the THUNDERBOLT attack.............

Let the govt pass some laws so that
the children can enjoy the rain without Parent's
Permission ....

4. NOMADS IN UNIFORM

We made our nest , a home for a while
Walls that witnessed our laughter and tears ...
We Wander , NOMADS IN UNIFORM ...
NO home to call mine .

I left my mark , a scribbled NAME on the wall
A Moment's Claim ....
Stories untold of struggles , love and war .
PaCkInG and UnPaCkInG , a constant plight ..
This Nomadic journey takes us far and wide .

Like giant old trees with branches wide
these walls have seen , generations tide ...
I yearn to return to places past ..
To listen to walls , that hold memories so dear .

Like MOWGLI swinging free and light
I'd glide through the memories , PURE DELIGHT ....

5. MOON AND BEYOND

It's from the rhyme Twinkle Twinkle, I started to stare,
At the vast universe, with wonder and care.
I watch the stars twinkling, with a curious grin,
Who's up there? I wonder, maybe aliens within!

I read about astronauts, who soared through space,
And dream of landing on the moon's bright face.
I'm gonna be the first Indian, to step on the moon's floor,
I'll plant a flag that says, "India's awesome, forevermore!"

I'll pack some samosas, and spicy chai too,
For a snack on the moon, that's what I'll do!
I'll dance like a superstar, in my spacesuit so bright,
And shout "Yay! I'm on the moon!" with all my might.

Twinkle, twinkle, little star, I'm coming to visit you,
With my rocket ship, and my astronaut crew!

We'll have some fun, in the moon's low gravity spin,
And make some moon memories, that will make
everyone grin!

6. A LUXURY SO RARE

The road unwinds, a journey's tale,
With Mom and Dad, my heart's set sail.
Thattukada's chai, a flavor so true,
A perfect blend of love, made just for you.

Sizzling hot, with foam so fine,
The creamy brown hue, a taste divine.
In the cup, a story unfolds,
Of moments cherished, young and old.

We three, a cup of tea, a luxury so rare,
A bond of love, beyond compare.
With every sip, our hearts revive,
In the warmth of chai, our spirits thrive.

Long drives, memories we create,
With chai's comfort, our souls participate.
No Starbucks charm, can match this vibe,
A family's love, in every cup, we imbibe.

Mom's smile, Dad's laughter, and I by their side,
Chai's magic, our hearts entwined.
In this simple joy, our love does reside,
A treasured moment, forever to abide.

7. BIRDS' PRIDE

Birds, with wings of vibrant hue,
Soar high, their beauty shining through.
Playing hide and seek, behind the rainbow's arc,
They rule the sky, with grace and embark.

Fashion designers of the air, they spread,
Their colorful plumage, a wondrous thread.
From peacocks' pride to eagles' mighty roar,
Olympians of the sky, they soar.

If only I could be a bird, free and wild,
I'd ride the wind, with a gentle, effortless glide.
But still, I'll marvel at their majesty and might,
And let their beauty be my guiding light...

8. WONDERS

In awe, I stand, before the world's great stage
Where wonders beckon and hearts turn the page...

The Eiffel Tower, an iron lady so grand
A testament in the heart of France's land
Shah Jahan's devotion.............
The Taj Mahal, a wonder, where love will never depart
A symbol of eternal love, a tomb for his queen
Forever serene...............
In London's beating heart, Big Ben's chimes resound
The world's largest clock, marking time,
without a bound.......................
Like Michael Jackson's magic, defying gravity's hold
The Leaning Tower of Pisa,
A marvel to behold........................
And in the deserts of Egypt, the Pyramids stand tall
A 3D triangle, of ancient math, for one and all...............

These wonders of the world, a treasure to behold
that never grow old.......................

9. Wah Chai !

In boiling water, ginger cracks its fiery soul,
Cardamom bursts ....
spilling joy into the rising steam.
Tea leaves unfurl like dancers in the swirl,
their dark essence bleeding into gold.
Sugar melts like snow........................
and milk pours in, soft and proud,
turning the tempest into velvet brown.............
yet the taste belongs not to milk alone,
but to the marriage of spice, leaf, and flame.

Chai is not merely a drink
it's a wonder brewed in clay cups and steel tumblers.....
No coffee with its bitterness, no mojito with its chill,
can dethrone the steaming elixir that rules every guest's
tray.

From the snows of Kashmir to the waves of
Kanyakumari,
chai spills across highways, hums in village courtyards,

glows in glass tumblers on railway platforms,
A perfect companion , Wah Chai !

10. MOSQUITOES' RHYME

When the moon shines bright up high,
Like a diamond in the sky,
No horns, no noise, the world asleep,
I curl in bed, my blanket deep.

But then they come — those tiny spies,
With buzzing wings and evil eyes!
Little vampires in the air,
They bite and bite — oh, life's not fair!

They give free injections, what a deal,
But make us sick — that's not ideal!
Their "Mmmmmm" song fills up the night,
No concert ever gave such fright!

We use sprays, we plug machines,
But still they come in sneaky scenes.
Good Night fails, All Out too,
They laugh and say, "We'll bite you, boo!"

Yet maybe they just want some fun,
Like us beneath the sleepy sun.
So let them buzz, just for a while —
Before I slap one with a smile! ☻

11. I'm a BIRIYANI LOVER

From north to south, all around,
Biriyani's smell can make me drown! 😨
Muradabadi—so soft and light,
One big plate and I'm alright! 🍱

Then comes Hyderabadi, super hot,
Spices dancing in the pot! 🌶
My tongue says "Help!" but still I eat,
Because that biriyani's hard to beat! 🍲

Thalapakkatti gives a punch,
Perfect biriyani for lunch! 🍴
And in Kerala, I must say,
Thalassery makes my day! 🌴

Malabar biriyani—so cool,
It makes me forget I'm late for school! 😋
Jeff biriyani from Yemen's place,
Brings a smile to my hungry face!

But best of all, I love the most,
Mummy's biriyani, she's the host! 👩‍🍳 💝
North and South in one big plate,
Her biriyani? Just too great! 🍲

So I shout loud, full of cheer,
"Biriyani! Come right here!" 📣
No pizza, burger, or mommos can win,
Because biriyani's my best friend within! 🍚 🔥

12. THE LOST RHYME

Jack and jill went up
The hill to fetch
A pail of water
But when they reached the hill-top well,
there wasn't a single drop of water.

Twinkle, twinkle
Little star
How i wonder, what you are
Up above the
The world so high
I've never seen you
In this smoky sky.

Ba ba black sheep
Have you any wool?
No sir, no sir
All the sheep's have died due to eating plastics .

Adults listen close,

If you don't progress
The rhymes you
Learnt will change
Like this and your future too.

13. MY ENGLISH GONE WRONG

I try to speak good English, yeah,
But words go crazy here and there! 😶
Teacher says, "Repeat it right!"
But my tongue just starts a fight! 👅

I said Na–ture for Nature cool,
Everyone laughed in my school! 😄
Then Pea–sand instead of Peasant came,
Now that word gives me shame! 🙈

I said Chole–store for Cholesterol,
Mummy said, "You selling chole roll?" 😶
And Pala–Payasam, my sweet treat,
Grandma said, "Oh, how cute, eat eat!"

Colonel looks like Co-lo-nel,
But they say "Kernel"! Is that a spell?? ⬚
Wednesday, why hide the "d"?
English letters just fooling me!

Then comes Often, I said Of-ten strong,
Teacher said, "The 't' is gone!" 💀
I said, "But ma'am, it's right there still!"
English rules just make me ill!

And Island—I said Is-land proud,
Everyone laughed so very loud! 🌴
They said, "The 's' is quiet, bro!"
Then why's it there? I'll never know!

Still I love this language fun,
Even if I say things wrong by ton!
Someday I'll speak it smooth and right...
But for now, I'll try my bite!

14. WAITING FOR FATHER'S CALL

Dad went sailing far away,
Where waves dance wild and winds play.
No Wi-Fi ....no signal ....
I keep on checking my silent phone.

I send him voice notes — laugh and cry,
When signal comes, they'll reach the sky.
Screenshots of video calls — my treasure chest,
When Dad comes home, that's our fest. ❤

No lights, no sweets on festival day,
Just his empty room where I lay ....
Mom smiles softly, hides her tears,
Counting tides instead of years.

No tech can beat the mighty sea,
But my heart sails where he'll be.
When his ship returns to land,
I'll run to hold his sailor hand. ⚓ 🐢

15. HOW I GOT MY NAME

My mom's an avid reader, you see,
She met Bhagavatha in a story ....
From Hayavadana by Girish Karnad,
She thought, "What a name! Simply applaud!"

Being a big fan of Lord Krishna divine,
She added Krishna—to make it shine.
A blend of books and Godly fame,
And that's how I got my fancy name!
A blend of Literature and spirituality ....

But here's the twist (oh, what a scene!),
Her Bhakti mode turned full routine—
"Eda Krishna! Poda Krishna!" all day long,
Guess her love comes with a yelling song! 🎵 😁

So while my name sounds holy and sweet,
It's shouted loud on every street!
Colloquial Bhakti at its peak.........................

16. AMMACHI MY QUEEN

When I think of her, I see her face,
so calm, so kind, so full of grace.
Her appam mutta curry fills the air,
with yummy smells beyond compare!

She tells me stories, old and sweet,
of her childhood days and garden neat.
When she dresses me for school each day,
I look extra nice — in every way!

Her avil mix — my favourite treat,
crunchy, tasty, oh so sweet!
Ammachi has conquered all my senses,
her love breaks all life's fences.

She inspires me in all I do,
Ammachi, my QUEEN — forever true!

17. TO MY DARK FANTASY

Hi my Dark Fantasy, my hero, my guide,
With you by my side, I felt the world wide.
Your hands — that strong and gentle hold,
Were the safest lock I'll ever behold.

With every walk, you showed me more,
The world beyond our little door.
Train rides, chocolates, Yummy parippu vada too,
Every simple thing felt new with you.

I'd wait for your visits, day by day,
To check your shirt pocket — my favorite way.
A Munch, a coin, a sweet surprise,
And that sparkle smiling through your eyes.

You'd drop a penny in my tiny bag,
And laugh when I'd boast and brag.
You taught me chess, those clever moves,
And showed how patience always proves.

I'd try to tease — you'd always win,
With that calm, wise grin within.
You never needed words to show,
The love your silence made me know.

But the hardest part, it breaks me still,
Is saying goodbye down that hill.
As I leave your home, my heart feels tight —
Because Dark Fantasy,
You are my light, Dear Appa . ꙅ³

18. A BAG OF PEDIGREE AND PAW PRINTS

You left too soon, my furry friend,
Your love had no beginning, no end.
Now by your bowl I sit and cry,
As days just fade, and time goes by.

No more wagging tail goodbyes,
No more furry hugs or cries,
No more bouncy playful streaks,
No more mischief in your cheeks.

A bag of Pedigree still lies near,
Half full of love, half full of tear.
You're gone — yet somehow still with me,
In every breath, in memory.

19. WHO AM I ?

In class he walks, cool and free,
With a smile so wide, it's a mystery!
Homework missing? He doesn't care —
Still grins like a billionaire! 😎

Teacher says, "Where's your note?"
He smiles so big, she forgets the quote!
Even when scolded, he stands so proud,
His laugh echoes — way too loud! 😁

Bench partner says, "Bro, exam's near!"
He just smiles, "Relax, my dear!"
Books may cry, pens may run,
But this boy's laughter weighs a ton!

PT period — his favorite hour,
He runs like Flash with extra power!
Maths class? Oh, that's his doom —
Still, he smiles across the room! 🏃

Lunch bell rings — his face goes bright,
He opens his box like it's pure delight!
Sharing snacks, cracking jokes all day,
Making school feel like a holiday!

So hats off to the smiling guy,
Who keeps the classroom's spirits high.
If happiness had a school ID,
It'd surely be — this boy's selfie! 📷 😁

20. CORONA DAYS

Metro city that never slept,
Suddenly fell into a hush so deep —
No honking cars, no crowded lanes,
Just echoes of silence and whispers of pain.

From my window at Palam Bagh, I'd stare,
At roads once alive, now empty and bare.
Dust hung still where laughter used to run,
The sky looked pale, hiding the sun.

Men with tired feet and broken dreams,
Walked miles back to their village streams.
Bags on shoulders, eyes filled with tears,
They carried their hunger, their hopes, their fears.

No school bells rang, no children's cheer,
Only the sound of sirens near.
Ambulances wailed through the street,
Carrying stories too heavy to repeat.

A quarantine building rose beside,
Where masked faces tried and tried,
To fight a war they couldn't see —
A battle between death and humanity.

Yet amidst the sorrow, a truth did bloom,
That love survives even in gloom.
When hands couldn't meet, hearts still prayed,
And kindness — not fear — quietly stayed.

These were the days that taught us all,
How fragile we stand, how quick we fall.
But from that silence, we learned to rise,
To value the breath, the tears, the skies. 🍃

21. ALLERGY TALES

My nose is a waterfall — nonstop flow,
Doctor says, "Immunity's low!"
Mom sighs, Dad rolls his eyes,
Tissues vanish like French fries!

To Dr. Krishnan I was sent,
(Oh wow — same name! Coincidence!)
He smiled and said, "Let's start the test!"
Then pricked my hand — not my best rest!

Tiny dots, one by one,
Guess who won? Dust mites — done!
They threw a party on my skin,
Saying, "We're the champs! Let's begin!"

Sprays, pills, therapy too,
Tried them all — nothing new.
My nose still runs its daily race,
Like a marathoner in first place!

But through the sneezes and the fun,
I found a friend — Dr. Krishnan!
We laugh each time the tissues fly,
"Bless you!" echoes to the sky! 😊